The College Mindfulness
Workbook

Elizabeth Catanese
Kate Sanchez
Community College of Philadelphia

Kendall Hunt
publishing company

Kendall Hunt
publishing company

www.kendallhunt.com
Send all inquiries to:
4050 Westmark Drive
Dubuque, IA 52004-1840

ISBN 978-1-7924-6193-4

Published in the United States of America

In memory of Barbara Auletta and Rose Fruscione
—EC

For Cesar and Millie
—KS

And with gratitude to Matt Blue and Karen Fleckenstein, as well as the entire Kendall Hunt team, for their artistry, author-focus, and good humor; to Sharon Thompson and Judy Gay, for believing in and supporting this project in its very first days at Community College of Philadelphia; to Maud, for always offering us guidance and coffee; and to our students, for inspiring us every day.

CONTENTS

INTRODUCTION: MINDFULNESS, EDUCATION, AND YOU

Mindfulness has become a popular word in American culture, and mindful activities abound around us. Adult coloring books line the shelves of superstores. Yoga classes are offered at most gyms. And doctors prescribe meditation as a stress-reduction tool. Even businesses, sports organizations, and schools are using mindfulness to improve overall health, focus, and achievement. Mindfulness has begun to infiltrate our lives from different angles, and it can be confusing to understand what it means and how it affects you. Though our associations, and perhaps stereotypical notions, about mindfulness may involve someone sitting cross-legged, chanting, and reaching absolute peace, it can be a lot simpler and more accessible than that to practice.

The goal of this workbook is to relate mindfulness to your lives, not only as students, but also as employees, family members, caretakers, friends, and all the other roles you may play in your life. Over the years, we've talked to students about what has been challenging during their time in college and configured this book to address those needs. We hope that by spending a small amount of time each week on activities in the workbook, you will reap many benefits.

WHAT IS MINDFULNESS?

Jon Kabat-Zinn, who started the Mindfulness-Based Stress Reduction program at the University of Massachusetts Medical Center, defines mindfulness as "paying attention in a particular way: on purpose, in the present moment, and nonjudgmentally" (4). This quotation serves as a great checklist for your own mindfulness practices.

- ▶ Are you being intentional about what you are focused on?

- ▶ Are you rooted in the now, or is your mind thinking about the past or future?

- ▶ Are you remaining objective, or are you judging your experience as good or bad?

The Mindfulness in Schools Project further explains, "Rather than worrying about what has happened or might happen, [mindfulness] trains us to respond skillfully to whatever is happening right now, be that good or bad" ("What is Mindfulness?"). This acceptance of present feelings or circumstances can be interpreted by many as "passivity or resignation"; however, "acceptance in this context refers to the ability to experience events fully, without resorting to either extreme of excessive preoccupation with, or suppression of, the experience" (Keng et al.). Are you able to root your attention in the present moment without reacting to it?

HISTORY OF MINDFULNESS

Though mindfulness may seem like a fresh topic, or may be completely new to you, people have been practicing mindfulness all over the globe for thousands of years, and it has been an integral part of Hindu, Buddhist, Christian, Jewish, and Muslim practices, seeing rises in popularity in the Middle Ages and in the last fifty years. There is not one way to be mindful, so practices have ranged from meditation to yoga to qi gong. In the 1950s and '60s, Zen Buddhism brought mindfulness back into popularity and influenced its increased popularity in psychology in the subsequent decades. Today, mindfulness and meditation are used to treat numerous health conditions, including chronic pain, anxiety, and depression, just to name a few (Keng et al.).

MINDFULNESS AND EDUCATION

In the last few decades, mindfulness has become an influential part of higher education; there is even an organization called the Association for the Contemplative Mind in Higher Education. They organize conferences and professional development to help faculty incorporate more mindfulness into the classroom or college campuses. Many colleges and universities have their own mindfulness contingent, with groups of college staff, faculty, and administration who meditate together or create mindfulness-related programming. Many faculty members also do mindfulness activities with their students to encourage focus, perseverance, and motivation.

Over the past fifty years, many researchers have studied mindfulness and its benefits, first from a medical or psychological standpoint, and more recently from the perspective of student success and well-being. In 2011, the team of Shian-Ling Keng, Moria J Smoski, and Clive Robins reviewed decades of mindfulness studies and found a plethora of benefits, including "life satisfaction," "agreeableness," "self-esteem," "empathy," as well as improvements with "depression," "anxiety," and "rumination," among others. The fact that mindfulness has been around so long also speaks to its ability to bolster humanity.

When Johns Hopkins University, Penn State University, and the Holistic Life Foundation teamed up for a study in 2010, they found that students in Baltimore, Maryland, benefited greatly from mindfulness programming. They saw improvement with completion rates, "behavior changes," improved "focus" and "calm," and better "stress regulation." Their article suggests, "Mindfulness-based approaches may be advantageous to urban youth by improving their capacity to cope with persistent stress. Enhancing responses to stress and the ability to control negative feelings and troubling thoughts . . . has the potential to benefit young people in school, at home and with friends, in the community, and throughout life" (Mendelson et al.).

Similarly, the Quiet Time program studied students and mindfulness in a San Francisco Middle School. They found that students showed more persistence, fought less frequently, and maintained better emotional health. A *New York Times* article even suggests meditation could lessen the achievement gap between schools in poorer neighborhoods with less resources and more affluent, suburban schools (Rosenthal).

MINDFULNESS AND YOU

Now that you know a bit more about the history and benefits of mindfulness, we wish you much success in creating a practice that works for you! Keep in mind that mindfulness, like anything you learn, takes time, patience, and practice. By checking in at least once each week with this workbook, you can gain some momentum. There is no experience or training necessary to use this book. Your teacher may assign certain pages, but you are also free to work on them, color them, or annotate them on your own. Give it a try, and see what happens. We hope this will be a positive experience for you, and that you will reap some practical benefits from this ancient, yet still very relevant, practice.

TESTIMONIALS

Our main inspiration for creating this workbook has been our own students who have benefited from the mindfulness work we've done with them in class. Students have shared that mindfulness practices have helped them in school, at work, at home, and in their personal relationships. They put mantras on their refrigerators, teach their BFFs to meditate, and focus on their breath when stressed out. Don't take our word for it, though! Read their testimonials below:

> Most of the time, I do not stop to make time for myself. I am a working mom, going to college, failing at cleaning and cooking, and sometimes so stressed I can't think straight. When I was given the task for class to stop and take a look inside my own head I was wary. Was it going to be worth the effort? As it turns out, I really needed to take this look at what my mind was thinking when I wasn't listening. I honestly opened up *The College Mindfulness Workbook* thinking that it was going to be some random pictures to color and some meditation things to say to myself. I was convinced that I should not waste too much time and just get it over with. I was surprised that very quickly I was becoming very interested as to what my own answers to some of these challenges would be. I was curious about what was

in my own head. Shouldn't I already know what my answers would be? Shouldn't I know what stresses me out or what's the most important thing to me right now? Shockingly enough, I didn't know. I think another lesson was that it's okay to just enjoy doing something fun, like coloring the sun. I am very glad that I decided to take this trip. Thank you very much to the wonderful authors who took their time to do this for their students. This book could benefit so many lives if people would just take the time out to stop and open it.

—Stephanie Murray

Without these mindfulness excercises, I would probably be struggling to get my mind back on track. Our normal is on hiatus due to COVID-19; catastrophe's happening with violence and protests and other issues that have made this year difficult to bargain with! I especially enjoyed the coloring pages in this workbook. Reflecting while doing the coloring pages, I realized that coloring reminded me of good old times when I enjoyed art. Every day, I would color one page a day to calm myself down from all the schoolwork and other important duties that needed to be taken care of. To be able to have the ability to do so without being criticized was important. I understand criticism is valuable to learn and improve skills that can come in handy in the future, but sometimes I feel like it takes the pressure off not to be criticized! While doing these coloring pages, I felt happy doing them! I reminded myself that I'm adequate and can accomplish my goal path. I was today years old when I found that colors can represent feelings such as happiness and anger. For me, I didn't color based on my feelings, I colored because again that's what I loved to do!

—Bryant Lane

The activity [from *The College Mindfulness Workbook*] that encouraged me to snap back into reality is living with intention. Living with purpose is essential because it enables us to create and achieve one goal rather than creating a list of goals that can crowd our minds. These past few days, my goal has been to stay focused. I chose this goal because I get distracted easily, and I overthink, and I wanted to give my mind a break and focus on staying on top of my studies. By telling myself to "stay focused," I noticed that my thoughts were slowing down, and it gave me the control to stay productive with tasks that were important to me. For instance, when I wake up, I have a habit of checking my phone and scrolling through Instagram, and I know that doing that does not benefit me. Yet by mentally telling myself to stay focused, I managed to put my phone down and stay productive with my studies. Practicing mindfulness can help people develop better relationships with themselves and improve life satisfaction. And this activity book is an excellent foundation to provide people with insight into restructuring their minds because it has helped me gain awareness of my thoughts and emotions. Though I am still trying to figure out how to process these thoughts, I enjoyed connecting with myself. And I find it interesting how we can reprogram our minds to view life from a different perspective by practicing mindfulness techniques.

—Phelire Banda

After completing the gratitude assignment in the mindfulness workbook, I learned I am most grateful for my life, health, and strength, my children, my husband, and my job. This year has been very stressful and unpredictable. So many lives were lost and depression is at its highest. Sometimes things get overwhelming and I see no way out, but these mindfulness assignments allow me to ponder the way things are, and they give me solutions for how I'm going to move on from here. What I am learning from these exercises is how to control stress. In my opinion, it is so important to take control of your thoughts and to keep your mind clear of negativity. I'm also learning to think of the positive things in my life and not to focus on what's going on around me that's out of my control. Being mindful matters so much to my wellbeing, and being optimistic in negative situations will help change my perspective on life as I continue school.

—Latifa Barnes

1

BEGINNING

Life is filled with beginnings. We experience life in a series of seasons and cycles. With the end of something, comes the beginning of something else. Night falls, but we wake to a sunny morning. Summer ends, but we are invigorated by the crispness of fall. Vacation ends, but we rise to the challenges of a new semester.

Sometimes we resist the end of something good or can't wait to start something new. Take a moment to notice how you feel about new beginnings in your academic life. Allow any emotions or thoughts that arise to just be there, and feel free to share them with others.

Remember that in any given moment, you can make a choice to start again: take a breath, set a goal, and move forward with renewed energy. Any good momentum you create now will flow into all your tasks ahead!

SELF-ASSESSMENT

Circle your response to the question below.

How calm are you, on a scale from 1 to 10, with 1 being very stressed and 10 being very calm?

1   2   3   4   5   6   7   8   9   10

What thoughts or feelings did you notice when reading the introduction to this chapter or filling out this self-assessment question? If you'd like, feel free to get more specific by writing or drawing what is going on for you in school and life right now:

LIVE WITH INTENTION

The first step to achieving a goal is creating one! One way to practice mindfulness in your classes or everyday life is to work with intentions. An intention is simply something you intend to do, a goal. However, by choosing just one thing to focus on each class period, day, or even week, you may notice quicker progress, focus, clarity, self-improvement, or even improved inner peace.

So how does it work? Simply write one intention you have in the chart below, along with the date (so you can reflect later). It's important that you just pick one thing, instead of overwhelming yourself with multiple goals. Your intention is very personal to you, so pick something just for you. For example, your intention could be to participate more in class discussions, review notes after class for ten minutes, or even develop connections with your classmates.

As you go through your day or week, reread your intention quietly or out loud to remind yourself of this focus. Inevitably, at some point, your brain will begin to focus on something else: your frustration with work, your growling stomach, maybe even your fun night ahead! This is okay and normal. However, if you notice this happens, bring yourself back to your intention. If you find it helpful to write intentions, come back to this page to write more later, or use the journal section of this book for more intentions.

DATE INTENTION

ENGAGE YOUR SENSES!

Practicing mindfulness often begins by paying attention through one of your senses. Small acts, such as smelling a flower, listening to the hum of your fan, or tasting your peppermint tea, can help you to get out of your thought cycle and into the now. Practicing moving from thoughts to the present moment through your senses will help you create a foundation for future mindfulness exercises.

For this exercise, you are going to engage one of your senses: choose either the sense of hearing or touch. Close your eyes and be silent for approximately two minutes. (You can set a timer if that's helpful.) In those two minutes: listen to all the sounds that you hear **or** feel the texture of as many nearby objects as you can.

After two minutes, use the box below to write down as many sounds as you can remember or a description of all the textures that you felt. If you prefer images to words, you can instead draw your sensory experiences.

CLASSROOM CENTERING POSES

Many people who practice mindfulness begin with the act of centering. Taking a moment to center before studying or entering a classroom can have a huge impact on your focus, as it helps you avoid carrying excess thoughts and stress into your next task.

In class or at home, hold the poses below for as long as you are able, or watch your friends or classmates hold the poses below. Do only what you are physically able to do, and modify the poses as needed. It's not only okay, but even desirable, to laugh while you're doing it! The idea is not to achieve a perfect yoga pose. The idea is simply to move your body.

After the activity, take a moment of silence before moving on. If an emotion or thought comes up during this process, write it down.

Image Adapted © nasharaga/Shutterstock.com

© NikVector/Shutterstock.com

COLOR THIS PAGE

Coloring is a mindfulness activity that many people find calming and inspiring. Color this page with any writing utensils you may have, or doodle inside the letters. As you color, think about the words on the page and all that is possible for you! What possibility can you take a first step toward today?

MINDFULNESS READING

Prairie Spring
by Willa Cather

Evening and the flat land,
Rich and sombre and always silent;
The miles of fresh-plowed soil,
Heavy and black, full of strength and harshness;
The growing wheat, the growing weeds,
The toiling horses, the tired men;
The long empty roads,
Sullen fires of sunset, fading,
The eternal, unresponsive sky.
Against all this, Youth,
Flaming like the wild roses,
Singing like the larks over the plowed fields,
Flashing like a star out of the twilight;
Youth with its insupportable sweetness,
Its fierce necessity,
Its sharp desire,
Singing and singing,
Out of the lips of silence,
Out of the earthy dusk.

Discussion Questions for Mindfulness Reading

1. Circle any words that you feel connect to something new or starting again.
2. How do spring and dusk symbolize "beginning" in the poem?

3. What specific beginnings are you experiencing right now? How do you feel about them?

QUOTATION TO CONTEMPLATE

"You can't cross the sea merely by standing
and staring at the water."

(Rabindranath Tagore)

1. What does this quotation mean literally?[1]

2. What is its deeper meaning?

3. What personal connections do you have with the quotation?

---

1. Literally means exactly or actually; without applying deeper analysis.

2

CREATING SPACE AND TIME

Do you ever feel like there aren't enough hours in a day? Or like you need more space to think, study, or just be? Finding time and space can be a major obstacle for students! With busy lives and bottomless studying, it can be difficult to organize your day and find a moment of quiet. Through mindfulness, however, you can find new ways to create space and time, and, in turn, build a foundation for success.

Sometimes just taking steps to remove the clutter from your desk, your calendar, and your mind can make a big difference. And cultivating a good relationship to space and time can make for a happier and healthier life in college.

SELF-ASSESSMENT

Circle your response to the question below.

How calm are you, on a scale from 1 to 10, with 1 being very stressed and 10 being very calm?

1 2 3 4 5 6 7 8 9 10

What thoughts or feelings did you notice when reading the introduction to this chapter or filling out this self-assessment question? If you'd like, feel free to get more specific by writing or drawing what is going on for you in school and life right now:

STUDY SPACE

Sometimes the spaces where we study are not conducive to focusing and learning. Take a moment to think about where you study. What sounds do you hear? What do you think about or look at as you study? How does the atmosphere make you feel? In the rectangles below, list or draw three things that distract you while studying, and then take a deep breath into your belly and let it out slowly. Next, brainstorm three steps you will take to improve your study space.

Distractions:

Steps:

1.

2.

3.

HOW I SPEND MY TIME

Time has a way of slipping by, especially if you are juggling multiple tasks related to work, college, and family, and it's easy to lose track of how you spend your hours each day. Look at the sample pie chart below that shows how Juvon spends his time. Then make a pie chart of how you spend yours. Last, fill in the other pie chart with how you would like to spend your time.

How Juvon Spends His Time

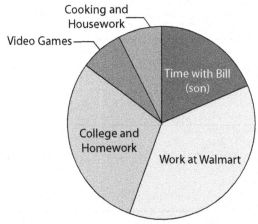

Source: Elizabeth Catanese and Kate Sanchez

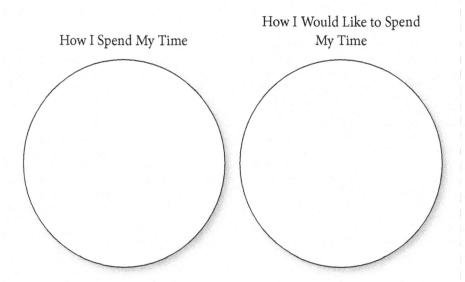

How I Spend My Time

How I Would Like to Spend My Time

MOVE

Have you ever spaced out while heading down the hall to class or while riding in the car? Sometimes we are so consumed by thoughts that we arrive and do not even remember the journey! We often move through our lives on autopilot and don't pay attention. This exercise asks you to focus simply on the act of moving, as a way of cultivating mindfulness of all the space and time you journey through each day.

Move slowly around the room for three minutes without talking. Notice what it feels like to move: Do you feel sensation in a particular part of your body? Do you notice something you hadn't before, or from a different perspective? What thoughts pop into your head? What do you notice about the space around you?

After three minutes of moving and noticing, reflect on how the exercise went below. Use the questions posed above as prompts if you get stuck.

MINDFUL MOMENT

Set a timer for two minutes. Close your eyes, and relax your body. Observe your thoughts during this time. When you are done, trace the person who best represents your thoughts. Were they related more to the past, present, or future? Then talk with someone else about your experience completing this exercise.

PAST   PRESENT   FUTURE

MINDFULNESS READING

From *The Sound of a Wild Snail Eating* by Elizabeth Tova Bailey

Inches from my bed and from each other stood the terrarium and a clock. While life in the terrarium flourished, time ticked away its seconds. But the relationship between time and the snail confused me. The snail would make its way through the terrarium while the hands of the clock hardly moved—so I often thought the snail traveled faster than time. Then, absorbed in snail-watching, I'd find that time had moved by, unnoticed. And what about the unfurling of a fern frond? Its pace was undetectable, yet day by day, it too, reached toward its goal.

The mountains of things I felt I needed to do reached the moon, yet there was little I could do about anything, and time continued to drag me along its path. We are all hostages of time. We each have the same number of hours and minutes to live within a day, yet to me it didn't seem equally doled out (37–38).

Discussion Questions for Mindfulness Reading

1. What images or pictures does the writer use to describe time passing? List them.

2. Reflect on time in your daily life. When does it move quickly or slowly?

3. Do you feel like we are "hostages of time"? How would you explain your relationship to time?

MEDITATION FOR A CALMER ATMOSPHERE

Read the meditation below, or have someone read it to you.

Take three deep breaths into your belly and out through your mouth with a sigh. Feel the stillness that already exists inside of you. Pause and breathe. Feel the stillness that already exists within this room. Take a deep breath and let it out. May this breath connect you with the sensations of your body.

Wiggle your fingers to represent the chaos that you have felt or are feeling in your life. Keep them moving. Now allow your hands to become still and peaceful. Feel the energy that remains in your hands, the energy of connection.

Pause for a moment and check in with your emotions. Is there anything inside that is causing you to feel stressed? Breathe in. And breathe out.

Write down your thoughts about how you can achieve a greater sense of peace.

3

CONSTRUCTING RELATIONSHIPS

The old adage "it takes a village" definitely applies to college students. You are connected to a network of professors, peers, and support services at the college or university, and a network of family, friends, and coworkers in your personal life. Though the village is there already, mindfulness can help you understand how to engage and connect with the rich resources found in these relationships.

A classmate or professor may help you in a difficult moment, and you also have the capacity to support them with your unique talents. As Carl Jung once wrote, "The meeting of two personalities is like the contact of two chemical substances: if there is any reaction, both are transformed." As you explore the relationships and communities in your life, stay open to the possibilities of connection.

SELF-ASSESSMENT

Circle your response to the question below.

How calm are you, on a scale from 1 to 10, with 1 being very stressed and 10 being very calm?

1 2 3 4 5 6 7 8 9 10

What thoughts or feelings did you notice when reading the introduction to this chapter or filling out this self-assessment question? If you'd like, feel free to get more specific by writing or drawing what is going on for you in school and life right now:

YOUR PROFESSOR'S GOALS FOR YOU

Write three specific goals your professor has for you:

1.

2.

3.

Check in with a partner to see how similar your answers are. Then discuss with your professor and classmates. You might even drop by during office hours to discuss this further.

Were you right about your professor's goals for you?

YES

SORTA

No

MINDFULNESS AT WORK

Most students have the goal of a specific future career, and many students work while taking classes. Thinking about ways to apply mindfulness at work can help you better connect with your coworkers, customers, and supervisors, but it can also help you make a positive impact through your profession. List three ways you could use mindfulness in your current or future job/career to make an impact and create relationships.

1.

2.

3.

TEAMWORK CENTERING POSE

Centering is an important mindfulness practice to help with focus and attention, but when completed with another person, it can also help to build connection. Just meditating (or even studying) in the same room as another can shift the energy in a positive, focused way. In class or at home, hold the pose below for as long as you are able, or watch your friends or classmates hold the pose. Do only what you are physically able to do, and modify the pose as needed. It's not only okay, but even desirable, to laugh if that feels right!

After the activity, reflect about the process or simply take a moment of silence before moving on. If an emotion or thought comes up during this process, write it down.

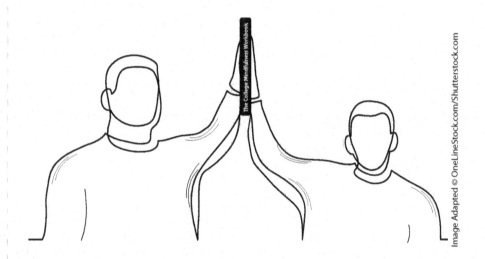

Image Adapted © OneLineStock.com/Shutterstock.com

CONNECTIONS TESSELLATION

A tessellation is a repeated geometric pattern with shapes that fit together seamlessly. Color the *connections tessellation* below. You can use anything to color it (crayons, highlighters, markers), or simply doodle inside the shapes to the fill the spaces. Then if you want (or are instructed to), rip your tessellation out of this book and connect it with another person's (or people's) tessellation. Discuss how the tessellation pages connect with each other. How are your artistic choices similar? How are they different?

MINDFULNESS READING

Discussion Questions for Mindfulness Reading

1. What do you notice about the relationship between the characters in the graphic novel panel?

2. How can you connect to this image or the words or both?

3. What makes constructing relationships difficult in our world? What makes it easy?

MEDITATION FOR COMMUNITY

Try to complete this meditation with at least one of your classmates. You might be on campus together, on a video call, or even just on the phone. Choose someone to read it aloud. The reader should pause for a few seconds between sentences. If you are alone, think about your classmates while you read it aloud.

Feel your feet against the floor. Take a deep breath in and slowly let it out.

May my classmates realize today and every day their value in this class and at the college as a whole.

May they feel the privilege of education at the same time they feel its profound difficulty.

May they understand that their persistence is beautiful.

May my classmates recognize and support each other however they can.

Write any thoughts you have here:

In a single word, how do you feel?

4

CULTIVATING GRATITUDE

Gratitude is a mindfulness practice that can completely change your perspective. American author Melody Beattie aptly remarks, "Gratitude unlocks the fullness of life. It turns what we have into enough, and more. It turns denial into acceptance, chaos to order, confusion to clarity. It can turn a meal into a feast, a house into a home, a stranger into a friend." Researchers echo this sentiment and have even concluded that being grateful can make us happier.

Cultivating gratitude as a mindfulness practice takes time and patience, much like nurturing a plant, as it changes the way you process your experiences and shifts your mindset. But in the end, all the digging and watering can boost your well-being.

SELF-ASSESSMENT

Circle your response to the question below.

How calm are you, on a scale from 1 to 10, with 1 being very stressed and 10 being very calm?

1 2 3 4 5 6 7 8 9 10

What thoughts or feelings did you notice when reading the introduction to this chapter or filling out this self-assessment question? If you'd like, feel free to get more specific by writing or drawing what is going on for you in school and life right now:

DRINKING GRATITUDE

As simple as it may seem, listing things you are grateful for has power! It forces you to shift your mindset and can even give you a positive boost.

© Kuznetsova Darja/Shutterstock.com

List three things in your life that you are grateful for:

1.

2.

3.

GRATEFUL FOR LEARNING

Write in response to the following prompt:

What lessons have you learned throughout your educational journey that you are grateful for?

EXPRESS YOUR GRATITUDE!

Choose one of the two options below, and then express your gratitude to another person. Feel free to use the journal pages at the end of this book if you need more space for completing the activity.

1. Write an e-mail thanking a teacher, mentor, friend, or family member for something they helped you with recently or in the past.

2. Write a 300-word gratitude statement to someone, and then read it out loud to them.

Brainstorming Space

List some people you are grateful for:

▶

▶

▶

Choose one individual from the list above, and circle the name. What has this person done to help you?

COLOR THIS PAGE

In Japanese culture, cherry blossoms represent the beautiful impermanence of life. Color the flowers in this *tree of gratitude* mindfully, with any writing utensils you have, or doodle inside the flowers. With each flower you color, think about a person in your life who is currently living for whom you feel a tremendous sense of gratitude.

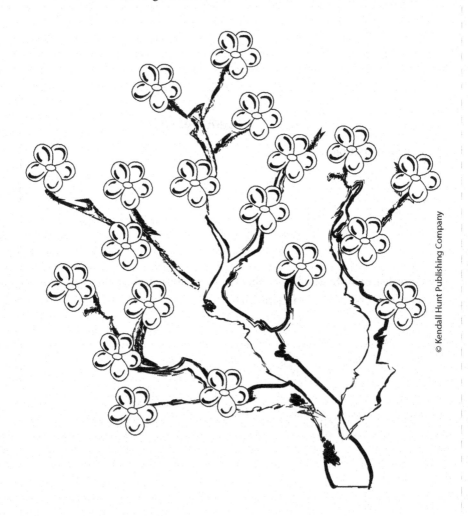

MINDFULNESS READING

From *The Alchemist* by Paulo Coelho

It was the time of day when all of Spain slept during the summer. The heat lasted until nightfall, and all that time he had to carry his jacket. But when he thought to complain about the burden of its weight, he remembered that, because he had the jacket, he had withstood the cold of the dawn.

We have to be prepared for change, he thought, and he was grateful for the jacket's weight and warmth. The jacket had a purpose, and so did the boy. His purpose in life was to travel, and after two years of walking the Andalusian terrain, he knew all the cities of the region.

Discussion Questions for Mindfulness Reading

1. What does the "jacket" symbolize in this excerpt?

2. Are there things you carry around, whether physical things, thoughts, or emotions, that feel like a burden at times? If so, list them. Do they serve a purpose in your life?

3. What does this excerpt teach readers about gratitude?

QUOTATION TO CONTEMPLATE

"I'm just very thankful. And I say that a lot because that's the most important message."

(Pharrell Williams)

1. What does this quotation mean literally?

2. What is its deeper meaning?

3. What personal connections do you have with the quotation?

5

COMMUNICATING

Words are powerful. A simple hello can build someone up, an angry outburst can tear someone down, and an unclear e-mail can leave everyone confused. Communication, whether online, over the phone, or in person, gives us power to express unique thoughts, clarify ideas, and even create relationships. Taking some time to mindfully construct your words can invigorate your overall learning experience and connect you with others in college.

Likewise, creating an intention to listen to others, without thinking about your next thought or judging another's opinion, can change the tone of the conversation. As writer Stephen R. Covey notices, "Most people don't listen with the intent to understand; they listen with the intent to reply." When you communicate with others, notice if you give them your full attention or if you are distracted by your own thoughts. Take a step back and see what happens.

SELF-ASSESSMENT

Circle your response to the question below.

How calm are you, on a scale from 1 to 10, with 1 being very stressed and 10 being very calm?

1 2 3 4 5 6 7 8 9 10

What thoughts or feelings did you notice when reading this introduction or filling out this self-assessment question? If you'd like, feel free to get more specific by writing or drawing what is going on for you in school and life right now:

BE MINDFUL OF OTHERS

Read and reflect on the definitions of the words *empathy* and *compassion*, and then answer the questions below.

Empathy "the feeling that you understand and share another person's experiences and emotions; the ability to share someone else's feelings"

Compassion "sympathetic consciousness of others' distress together with a desire to alleviate it"

(Definitions from Merriam-Webster Dictionary)

1. How do these terms relate to your experience in class?

2. How do the terms relate to your current or future job/career?

E-MAIL MINDFULLY

Communicating with your professors is critical in college, and oftentimes this correspondence takes place using e-mail. This is great because it's a quick way to communicate with your professor, but sometimes e-mails can take on an unintended tone or seem unclear to the recipient. Using mindfulness to construct your e-mails can help with this!

Read the tips below, and then give it a try! Mindfully write an e-mail to one of your professors. You can write to them about anything, including just to say you found a particular concept in class interesting.

1. **Get in the right head space.**
   Sometimes communication can be emotional, especially if you are e-mailing to dispute a grade or ask for an extension. Take a moment to pause and close your eyes. Take three deep breaths. Think of the professor you are writing this e-mail to and say hello to them in your mind.

2. **Be clear.**
   Try to write your thoughts and questions as clearly as possible, choosing the best words to express your point. After you write the e-mail, read over it and revise any words you're not sure about or sentences that seem confusing. Make sure the tone matches your intention.

3. **Be professional.**
   Open with a salutation, such as Dear Professor Papurt, edit your writing, and sign your name. Take time to be mindful of the basic parts of the e-mail. This may affect how your e-mail is received.

SMILE

Without talking, smile at three different people in the classroom. Nod to acknowledge that you have been smiled at. Do not leave your professor out of this activity! If you are in a space other than the classroom, try smiling at a person nearby or simply smiling at an object that you see.

Research has found that facial expressions can impact feelings, your own and others'. Reflect about how you felt while you were completing this activity and afterward.

INTERPRET TEACHER FEEDBACK

Take a look at the following two pieces of sample feedback, and write or discuss how you would feel if you were a student receiving each piece of feedback. In general, how do you feel when you receive feedback from an instructor? Do grades influence your ability to use feedback to improve? Explain.

Hi, Shamika.

I can tell from this essay how well you have been paying attention in class. Your thesis statement is very clear, and you make some compelling points in your essay. When you revise your essay, try to be even more specific in the examples you give to support your thesis statement. For expanding paragraphs, remember the "who, what, where, when, why" strategy we discussed. Please feel free to see me if you would like to discuss this further!

Draft Grade: **A–**

Hi, Shamika.

I can tell from this essay how well you have been paying attention in class. Your thesis statement is very clear, and you make some compelling points in your essay. When you revise your essay, try to be even more specific in the examples you give to support your thesis statement. For expanding paragraphs, remember the "who, what, where, when, why" strategy we discussed. Please feel free to see me if you would like to discuss this further!

Draft Grade: **D**

MINDFULNESS READING

Kriah

by Darla Himeles

The lake's been moaning
an earth-heavy groan
nightly, ice pushing
ice:

closed ears, listen.

Our goldenest word,
especially now—
heart contracting,
loosening, contracting—
is listen.

Mother is howling—
listen.

Discussion Questions for Mindfulness Reading

1. Humans can have difficulty receiving messages from mother earth, as this poem describes. Circle the words that emphasize this communication difficulty.

2. Why is "listen" described as "Our goldenest word"?

3. Do you ever feel like you are not being heard? What gets in the way of us being completely present and listening to others?

QUOTATION TO CONTEMPLATE

"When the whole world is silent,
even one voice becomes powerful."

(Malala Yousafzai)

1. What does this quotation mean literally?

2. What is its deeper meaning?

3. What personal connections do you have with the quotation?

6

PAYING ATTENTION

As you go through the day, you may have your backpack, ID, and coffee in tow, but you may also be carrying thoughts about your past or future. This makes it hard to focus on that sociology lecture or biology study guide or even this sentence! When thinking about the past or the future, people can lose their connection to the present. Writer Eckhart Tolle emphasizes this idea in *The Power of Now:* "Your outer journey may contain a million steps; your inner journey only has one: the step you are taking right now." By shifting attention to the present moment, we can increase productivity and engage with life in a deeper way.

Paying attention is a skill that we must hone, though. It takes practice! So, if you find yourself spacing out for a moment in class, just bring your attention back to the task at hand. And repeat. Eventually, you will be able to focus on the present for longer periods of time and reap the benefits of being in the now.

SELF-ASSESSMENT

Circle your response to the question below.

How calm are you, on a scale from 1 to 10, with 1 being very stressed and 10 being very calm?

1 2 3 4 5 6 7 8 9 10

What thoughts or feelings did you notice when reading the introduction to this chapter or filling out this self-assessment question? If you'd like, feel free to get more specific by writing or drawing what is going on for you in school and life right now:

MINDFUL PARAGRAPH/PROBLEM-SOLVING

Taking time to slow down and avoid rushing through your work will not only enhance learning, but may also help you avoid mistakes. Some people even report completing their work faster because they are not distracted by fixing their mistakes or rushing toward "the next thing." Practice slowing down by completing one of the exercises below, and then reflect on your experience. Go to the journal section of this book for space to complete this activity.

Mindful Paragraph Exercise

1. Write a paragraph one sentence at a time.

2. Pause for five to ten seconds between each sentence. Do this for five to seven sentences.

3. Read over your paragraph, and replace or add at least one word to make it more specific or precise.

4. Reflect on this experience of slowing down.

You may want to work from a prompt, such as:

- ▶ Write a paragraph about your progress in this course.

- ▶ Summarize the information presented in class today.

- ▶ Brainstorm ideas for an upcoming essay.

Mindful Problem-Solving Exercise

1. Complete a multistep problem one part at a time.

2. Pause for ten seconds between steps.

3. Look over the problem one last time, checking for mistakes.

4. Reflect on this experience of slowing down.

You may want to work from a math problem you have for a class or complete the algebra problem below by solving for x:

$$2x + 6 = 4x - 2$$

EMOTION SEARCH

This activity replicates the experience of emotions popping up at any moment. Sometimes it is helpful to pay attention to emotions, to find them in the midst of other thoughts, before taking action.

Circle the first emotion word you find in the following crossword puzzle. Then write an example of how that emotion has come up in your life. What are your feelings about that emotion?

Words

anger

anxiety

astonishment

despair

embarrassment

excitement

exhilaration

fear

grief

happiness

overwhelm

sadness

surprise

T	D	D	E	V	D	K	K	P	I	A	T	M	Y	R
R	S	R	A	N	X	I	E	T	Y	S	N	L	C	D
E	D	C	D	G	C	D	S	M	J	T	E	E	M	A
G	M	M	R	R	E	S	Y	B	T	O	M	H	U	H
H	L	I	E	S	E	H	V	D	F	N	E	W	U	K
W	E	G	P	N	R	T	T	B	H	I	T	R	X	N
F	N	A	D	Q	Y	D	L	Y	T	S	I	E	L	D
A	I	A	F	U	V	W	H	J	E	H	C	V	Y	G
R	S	Z	C	E	X	I	B	N	B	M	X	O	G	U
E	L	M	F	B	A	T	Z	J	R	E	E	X	T	G
D	D	E	X	S	Y	R	D	Q	B	N	V	I	F	Z
S	U	R	P	R	I	S	E	K	I	T	Y	T	X	J
T	N	E	M	S	S	A	R	R	A	B	M	E	Z	Z
E	X	H	I	L	A	R	A	T	I	O	N	R	Q	T
S	S	E	N	I	P	P	A	H	V	J	A	E	M	E

Created by Elizabeth Catanese using https://puzzlemaker.discoveryeducation.com/

COLOR YOUR FEELINGS

While paying attention to your emotions in the present moment, color the picture that most closely represents how you feel, or draw your own picture in the blank journal page section of this book. Remember you can use any writing implement to color or even doodle inside the shapes.

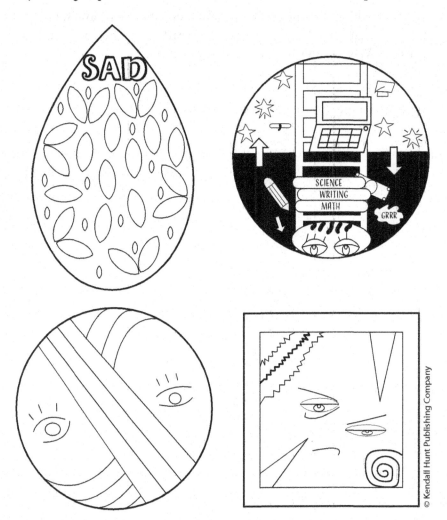

DRAW

The act of drawing requires a lot of mindfulness. You must pay close attention to what you see to replicate it. Though other factors like feelings and imagination may impact *how* you draw it, observing something carefully grounds you in this moment.

Draw something that you see for five minutes. Observe it closely, focusing not on the outcome but the process. It doesn't matter how your drawing turns out. What matters is that you paid attention.

MINDFULNESS READING

In the following excerpt from book 12 of *The Odyssey* by Homer, the character Circe instructs traveler Odysseus to pay attention to his journey and not be distracted by a dangerous temptation.

"So far so good," said she, when I had ended my story, "and now pay attention to what I am about to tell you—heaven itself, indeed, will recall it to your recollection. First you will come to the Sirens who enchant all who come near them. If any one unwarily draws in too close and hears the singing of the Sirens, his wife and children will never welcome him home again, for they sit in a green field and warble him to death with the sweetness of their song. There is a great heap of dead men's bones lying all around, with the flesh still rotting off them. Therefore pass these Sirens by, and stop your men's ears with wax that none of them may hear; but if you like you can listen yourself, for you may get the men to bind you as you stand upright on a cross-piece half way up the mast, and they must lash the rope's ends to the mast itself, that you may have the pleasure of listening. If you beg and pray the men to unloose you, then they must bind you faster."

Discussion Questions for Mindfulness Reading

1. What kind of temptation does Circe say Odysseus will encounter, and how does she suggest that he avoid that temptation?

2. What temptations get in the way of your ability to pay attention in college?

3. Name two strategies that can help you pay attention in a college class.

CLASS MEDITATION FOR FOCUS

Choose someone to read the following meditation at the start of class. The reader should pause for a few seconds after each sentence. If you are alone, you could use this before starting your homework or studying. Simply read the meditation to yourself, pausing between sentences.

The purpose of this short meditation is to help us move from our busy lives outside of college to this classroom, right here, right now.

Close your eyes, and if you feel comfortable with it, sit up in your chair. As your body gets still, focus on one simple truth: in this moment you are breathing. Do not try to change anything about your breathing; simply notice that it's happening. Feel your abdomen as it fills with air on the in-breath and then moves back toward your spine on the out-breath.

There is no need to do anything. There is no need to run an errand, take care of someone else; rush to a job, respond to that text, or to complete any of the tasks that may fill your day. You only have to be present here, in this moment. Keep breathing as we pause for about a minute of silence.

From time to time your mind will wander off into thoughts. Notice your mind wandering, and with love and kindness, bring it back to the flow of your breathing. You are here right now, simply being.

As you observe your breathing, you may notice sensations in your body. See if you can become aware of them. Feel your body from head to toe. Observe the sense of your body as a whole.

Be here with any feelings you may have as you continue to breathe. Simply notice them. In this moment you are simply being, simply noticing. Return to your breath.

You are human, complete and whole.

Slowly return to the classroom by opening your eyes and perhaps wiggling your fingers or toes. We will now focus on learning together.

7

EXPLORING YOUR PERSONALITY

College is a time of self-exploration. You find yourself in a new environment full of new challenges, away from the people who have shaped your life thus far. It is the perfect opportunity to reflect on who you are and how you can express yourself to the world in an authentic way.

As American author Henry David Thoreau puts it, "Not until we are lost do we begin to understand ourselves." So, use each obstacle and unmarked trail as a window into yourself. Pull back the curtains, peer inside, and be curious about what you find.

SELF-ASSESSMENT

Circle your response to the question below.

How calm are you, on a scale from 1 to 10, with 1 being very stressed and 10 being very calm?

1   2   3   4   5   6   7   8   9   10

What thoughts or feelings did you notice when reading the introduction to this chapter or filling out this self-assessment question? If you'd like, feel free to get more specific by writing or drawing what is going on for you in school and life right now:

WHO ARE YOU?

What does the word *personality* mean? What do you know about your personality traits? What academic subjects and careers fit well with your personality? In this chapter, you will reflect more about who you are. Write what you know already about who you are here! Be as honest as possible.

HELP YOUR CHICKENS TO HATCH!

As you explore your personality, it's important to acknowledge your individual potential, and then make space for it to grow in your life, constantly moving toward self-actualization.

Next to each egg, write a hidden skill or talent that you would like to nurture.

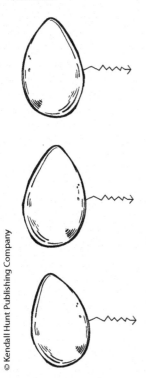

What is one step you can take to nurture a skill or talent?

HUMAN NATURE WALK

Go outside for ten to fifteen minutes. You might take a walk, or simply sit in the sunshine, as you contemplate the following question:

Are your personality and desires in alignment with what you plan to study in college?

It is extremely common in college to experience some conflict when contemplating this question. Is there a difference between what you want to do and what another person or other people want you to do? Is there a difference between what you want to do and what makes money? Are you experiencing a lack of clarity about what you want to do? Is there an academic requirement that stands in the way of your progress?

Allow whatever nature is on the outside (the air, trees, people, and so forth) to help you clarify your nature on the inside. After you complete this exercise, write some of your thoughts here. Then discuss your insights with someone else.

COLOR YOUR PERSONALITY

An enneagram is a circle chart that includes various personality types. While some people find personality charts frustrating (humans can be way more complicated than personality charts sometimes imply!), others find such charts to be a great starting point for contemplating what makes them tick. After reading the following descriptions, color (or doodle in) the enneagram type you relate to most. If you find this activity meaningful, go online to take a free enneagram personality test and learn more about nuances in the enneagram.

1. The reformer: rational, restrained, perfectionistic
2. The helper: caring, interpersonally-talented, loyal
3. The achiever: practical, driven, motivated by success
4. The individualist: expressive, symbol-maker, contemplative
5. The investigator: curious, intellectual, inventive
6. The loyalist: responsible, devoted, guarded
7. The enthusiast: playful, exuberant, spur-of-the-moment, scattered
8. The challenger: self-assured, strong-willed, determined
9. The peacemaker: courteous, agreeable, approachable, conflict-avoidant

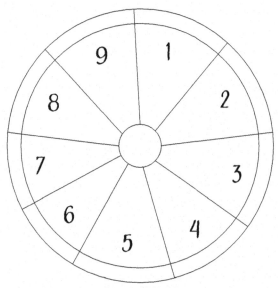

MINDFULNESS READING

Read each passage below and reflect on the personalities of the characters being described. What, in the passages, tips you off to the characters' personalities?

The personality of Sherlock Holmes:

From *Sherlock Holmes, A Case of Identity* by Arthur Conan Doyle

> "My dear fellow," said Sherlock Holmes as we sat on either side of the fire in his lodgings at Baker Street, "life is infinitely stranger than anything which the mind of man could invent. We would not dare to conceive the things which are really mere commonplaces of existence. If we could fly out of that window hand in hand, hover over this great city, gently remove the roofs, and peep in at the queer things which are going on, the strange coincidences, the plannings, the cross-purposes, the wonderful chains of events, working through generations, and leading to the most outré results, it would make all fiction with its conventionalities and foreseen conclusions most stale and unprofitable."

The personality of Momma:

From *Saavy* by Ingrid Law

> . . . *my* momma's cakes never lopped to the side or to the middle. Momma's cakes were perfect, just like Momma, because that was her saavy. Momma was perfect. Anything she made was perfect. Everything she did was perfect. Even when she messed up, Momma messed up perfectly.

Discussion Questions for Mindfulness Reading

1. Describe the personality of Sherlock Holmes. What, in the passage, led you to describe him in this way?

2. Describe the personality of Momma in *Saavy*. What, in the passage, led you to describe her in that way?

3. Now, imagine someone observing YOU. Write a sentence that describes your personality from a third-person point of view.

QUOTATION TO CONTEMPLATE

"I am of old and young, of the foolish as much as the wise/
Regardless of others, ever regardful of others,/
Maternal as well as paternal, a child as well as a man,/
Stuffed with the stuff that is coarse,
and stuffed with the stuff that is fine . . . "

(Walt Whitman in *Leaves of Grass*)

1. What does this quotation mean literally?

2. What is its deeper meaning?

3. What personal connections do you have with the quotation?

8

EMBRACING DIVERSITY

Some of the best teachers in life are people who are unlike you. Whether they were born in a different country, practice a different religion, or experience the world through a different racial identity, people who are unlike you can open your eyes to a different way of living and learning. Even diverse characters in books or media can open your mind to others' thoughts and experiences, and learning about these differences can help you be a more inclusive citizen. As Audre Lorde once emphasized, "It is not our differences that divide us. It is our inability to recognize, accept, and celebrate those differences" (L. Porter). Mindfulness provides an opportunity to reflect on our personal biases, as well as the opportunities around us to "recognize, accept, and celebrate" all people. Then, ideally, and together, we can bridge some of the divides that exist around us.

To truly embrace diversity, start by using one of the most basic mindfulness concepts: noticing. Be aware of what makes each person in your classroom and community unique. Then use your combined insights and strengths to learn and grow together.

SELF-ASSESSMENT

Circle your response to the question below.

How calm are you, on a scale from 1 to 10, with 1 being very stressed and 10 being very calm?

1 2 3 4 5 6 7 8 9 10

What thoughts or feelings did you notice when reading the introduction to this chapter or filling out this self-assessment question? If you'd like, feel free to get more specific by writing or drawing what is going on for you in school and life right now:

MAKE A LIST

Make a list of what you could gain by learning with or from someone who is different from you.

1.

2.

3.

4.

5.

CREATE AN IDENTITY PORTRAIT!

Create a realistic or symbolic self-portrait that reveals aspects of your identity. For example, if you identify as Polish American you might include a Polish flag and an American flag. If you identify as a member of the LGBTQ+ community, you might include a rainbow. If baking is a huge part of your identity, you might draw cookies for your eyes. Share your portrait with a partner and discuss similarities and differences in your identities.

DIVERSITY IN YOUR LIFE

Many people surround themselves with others who are like them, in their daily lives and communities, and even on their college campuses. This exercise asks you to think more about the people you interact with on a daily basis, as well as ways you could create opportunities to engage with others who are not like you in one way or another.

First, let's explore the difference between the following terms:

Culture: "the customary beliefs, social forms, and material traits of a racial, religious, or social group; the characteristic features of everyday existence (such as diversions or a way of life) shared by people in a place or time"

Race: "any one of the groups that humans are often divided into based on physical traits regarded as common among people of shared ancestry"

(Definitions from Merriam-Webster Dictionary)

Answer the following questions after some reflection on your personal experiences:

1. Which cultures and races do you interact with regularly? What is the nature of the interactions?

2. Brainstorm some ways you could interact with cultures and races different from the ones you encounter.

3. Do you experience enough diversity in your life? Explain.

WHERE WILL YOU GO?

Traveling can be a great way to experience the diversity of the human experience. Perhaps your college has a study-abroad program, or you plan to travel sometime after college, or you would like to learn about a place simply by reading about it. Color one of the locations listed on this page that you are interested in or write the name of a different place of interest that is not on the list. Then draw and color the flag of that place.

DRAW THE FLAG OF YOUR CHOSEN LOCATION HERE

CAMBODIA

MEXICO

ITALY

BELIZE

JAPAN

TANZANIA

MEDITATION FOR ACCEPTANCE

To complete this meditation, choose someone to read it aloud or simply read it to yourself. Pause for a few seconds between sentences.

Feel your body in this room. Sense others around you.

There may be aspects of yourself that you do not like. May you find self-acceptance for who you are, right here, right now.

In this world, many people are struggling to be who they are. May these people feel moments of peace and support.

Acceptance of difference can be scary. Acceptance of difference can be beautiful. May our efforts toward inclusion and acceptance create a brighter, kinder world.

When you are ready, open your eyes and open your hearts to the diversity around you.

QUOTATION TO CONTEMPLATE

"But all our phrasing—race relations, racial chasm,
racial justice, racial profiling, white privilege, even white
supremacy—serves to obscure that racism is a visceral
experience, that it dislodges brains, blocks airways,
rips muscle, extracts organs, cracks bones, breaks teeth.
You must never look away from this. You must always
remember that the sociology, the history, the economics,
the graphs, the charts, the regressions all land, with great
violence, upon the body."

From *Between the World and Me* by Ta-Nehisi Coates

1. What does this quotation mean literally?

2. What is its deeper meaning?

3. What personal connections do you have with the quotation?

9

BUILDING EMOTIONAL INTELLIGENCE

As a college student, you may experience a lot of stressors, from deadlines, to difficult professors, to personal issues. When these pile up you can experience cognitive overload, which can lead to anxiety, insomnia, and feeling overwhelmed. Mindfulness has the potential to break this overloaded cycle by forcing you to look inward and to identify and process emotion. It also can help you to be present when listening to others and to understand how they may be feeling.

SELF-ASSESSMENT

Circle your response to the question below.

How calm are you, on a scale from 1 to 10, with 1 being very stressed and 10 being very calm?

1   2   3   4   5   6   7   8   9   10

What thoughts or feelings did you notice when reading the introduction to this chapter or filling out this self-assessment question? If you'd like, feel free to get more specific by writing or drawing what is going on for you in school and life right now:

EMOTIONAL WELL-BEING SHOPPING LIST

It's easy to know what you need or want in terms of commodities. New shoes? New headphones? More milk for the fridge? Make a list of three items that you need or want for increased *emotional* well-being.

Here are some examples:

1. More time each week to rest

2. A friend who will listen to my problems

3. A sense that my son is happy

Now make your list:

1.

2.

3.

What's one step you could take to get one of the needs or desires met? If you can't think of one on your own, ask a partner!

1.

THOUGHT AND FEELING CHECK-IN

Close your eyes and check in with what you are thinking and feeling right now. Write down one feeling and one thought when you are ready:

1. Feeling→

2. Thought→

Where in your body are your feeling(s) located?

Are you comfortable checking in with your feelings? Why or why not?

FACIAL EXPRESSION CHALLENGES

Because body language plays such a huge role in communication, having emotional intelligence includes reading others' expressions. The body can say so much without uttering a single word. Try the challenges below. You might want to look in the mirror while you do them.

Challenges:

1. Smile with your eyes.

2. Frown with your eyebrows.

3. Reflect uncertainty with your mouth.

Then ask someone how they are. When they answer, be completely present, and notice their expression along with their words.

THE WEATHER IN MY BRAIN

DRAW IT HERE

MINDFULNESS READING

From **Walden** by Henry David Thoreau

However mean your life is, meet it and live it; do not shun it and call it hard names. It is not so bad as you are. It looks poorest when you are richest. The fault-finder will find faults even in paradise. Love your life, poor as it is. You may perhaps have some pleasant, thrilling, glorious hours, even in a poorhouse. The setting sun is reflected from the windows of the almshouse as brightly as from the rich man's abode; the snow melts before its door as early in the spring. I do not see but a quiet mind may live as contentedly there, and have as cheering thoughts, as in a palace.

Discussion Questions for Mindfulness Reading

1. What do you think Thoreau is asking you to do?

2. Reread the first sentence above. How can acceptance be a tool for emotional intelligence? Do you find that you accept all your emotions or push some away?

3. Can you remember a time when, looking back, things weren't as bad as you thought they were? What emotions does remembering this bring up for you?

QUOTATION TO CONTEMPLATE

"Holding on to anger is like grasping a hot coal
with the intent of throwing it at someone else:
you are the one who gets burned."

Buddhaghoṣa

1. What does this quotation mean literally?

2. What is its deeper meaning?

3. What personal connections do you have with the quotation?

10

PERSISTING

To persist is to continue, to move forward despite the circumstances. If you are living right now, you are already persisting! However, some people struggle more than others with persistence in their academic lives. What keeps some people going and stops others? This chapter brings awareness to the power of persistence in the face of challenges in college.

A reflective and mindful approach can increase your persistence skills and can help you notice the support systems you have now, as well as contemplate the kind of support you'll need in the future. Before beginning this chapter, think about any obstacles or challenges you have faced and have been able to overcome. What helped you get through these challenges?

SELF-ASSESSMENT

Circle your response to the question below.

How calm are you, on a scale from 1 to 10, with 1 being very stressed and 10 being very calm?

1   2   3   4   5   6   7   8   9   10

What thoughts or feelings did you notice when reading the introduction to this chapter or filling out this self-assessment question? If you'd like, feel free to get more specific by writing or drawing what is going on for you in school and life right now:

MY SUPPORT SYSTEM

One way to increase your persistence in college is to lean into your support system. Sometimes you may just need some encouragement or the resources another can provide.

Who is on your team? Color the soccer team jerseys below and label the jerseys with people who support you most in your educational journey right now. These could be relatives, roommates or classmates, teachers, or even book or TV characters who inspire you.

© mijatmijatovic/Shutterstock.com

MAKE A LIST: CHALLENGES AND SOLUTIONS

Below, make a list of some challenges you are facing right now. After making your list, take a deep breath and write your desired outcome for each challenge. Finally, write down one small step you can take toward overcoming each challenge.

Challenges

Example: I am failing math.

1.

2.

3.

Desired Outcomes

Example: I would like to pass math.

1.

2.

3.

Small Steps toward Desired Outcomes

Example: I am going to e-mail my teacher mindfully tonight to make an appointment with her.

1.

2.

3.

MOUNTAIN POSE

In yoga, mountain pose can help you achieve balance, strength, and a feeling of being firmly rooted to the earth. First, think about the associations you have with mountains. Do you see them as a symbol of strength? Can you notice how they are completely still despite the storms that blow by? Strike a mountain pose, standing or sitting, for two minutes or as long as you can hold it. Then write down the challenges you are facing that require the most strength.

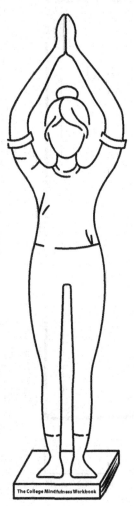

Image Adapted © ALX1618/Shuttetstock.com

The College Mindfulness Workbook

CONTAINMENT BOX

Write your hardest secret or struggle in the box below. If you are ready to reflect about it, leave it open. If it is too painful to reflect about it now, simply color over what you wrote. The box will hold your secret until you are ready to address it.

WRITE YOUR STRUGGLE HERE:

MINDFULNESS READING

Excerpt from **"What Suffering Does"** by David Brooks

Recovering from suffering is not like recovering from a disease. Many people don't come out healed; they come out different . . . Instead of recoiling from . . . loving commitments that almost always involve suffering, they throw themselves more deeply into them.

Discussion Questions for Mindfulness Reading

1. What words stand out to you the most in this excerpt? Circle them in the text and reflect on how they make you feel.

2. What does Brooks mean when he writes, "they come out different"?

3. How might Brooks's ideas about suffering impact the way you face a current obstacle?

QUOTATION TO CONTEMPLATE

"They tried to bury us.
They didn't know we were seeds."

(Mexican Proverb)

1. What does this quotation mean literally?

2. What is its deeper meaning?

3. What personal connections do you have with the quotation?

11

BEING WELL

Wellness is more than just keeping the body healthy. It takes a holistic approach to make sure your mind and body are healthy and in alignment. Many who have practiced yoga, ballet, or long-distance running can understand the deep connection between physical and mental health. Every movement strengthens the body while also training the mind. Likewise, this chapter focuses on strategies for cultivating overall wellness, with exercises to clear your mind, to motivate you, and to allow you to creatively express your state of mind.

SELF-ASSESSMENT

Circle your response to the question below.

How calm are you, on a scale from 1 to 10, with 1 being very stressed and 10 being very calm?

1 2 3 4 5 6 7 8 9 10

What thoughts or feelings did you notice when reading the introduction to this chapter or filling out this self-assessment question? If you'd like, feel free to get more specific by writing or drawing what is going on for you in school and life right now:

MIND-BODY HARMONY

Paying attention to both your mental and physical well-being are important to overall health, but sometimes people pay more attention to one than the other over time, or on a given day.

Where are you placing most of your attention today: mind or body?

What are you doing to nourish that aspect of your health?

What is one thing you could do to nourish the other part?

BRAIN DUMP

Do you ever feel like your brain is so full that you can't seem to clear it? Are you conscious of the thoughts that cycle through your mind? Do you ever lie down to sleep at night, only for thoughts to begin swirling? Sometimes writing down your thoughts can help you notice your thoughts, lessen your cognitive overload, and even help you sleep! This then can lead to improved overall wellness.

Over the course of a few minutes, use the space below to write down each thought that you have as it pops into your head. Allow the paper to hold the thoughts. When/if you have no thoughts, just notice what it feels like when your mind is clear.

BOOST YOUR MOOD WITH A SONG

Music, and its ability to make us move, has benefits for both physical and mental health, and the alignment of the two. Some practitioners even use music therapy for things like pain and anxiety.

Listen to a song that makes you feel happy for the sole purpose of experiencing a boost. If it moves you, feel free to dance along to the beat. You might also write lyrics below or draw images the song inspires.

FILL IN THE MANDALA

A mandala is a patterned shape that represents a small piece of the universe. The ritual of coloring mandalas can help you align mind and body by connecting the physical act of coloring or drawing with the mental act of creativity. Draw, doodle, or color in the mandala below. Fill it up with you!

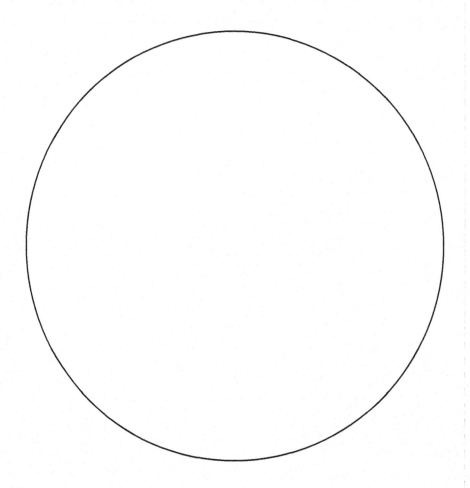

MINDFULNESS READING

WILD GEESE

You do not have to be good.
You do not have to walk on your knees
for a hundred miles through the desert, repenting.
You only have to let the soft animal of your body
    love what it loves.
Tell me about despair, yours, and I will tell you mine.
Meanwhile the world goes on.
Meanwhile the sun and the clear pebbles of the rain
are moving across the landscapes,
over the prairies and the deep trees,
the mountains and the rivers.
Meanwhile the wild geese, high in the clean blue air,
are heading home again.
Whoever you are, no matter how lonely,
the world offers itself to your imagination,
calls to you like the wild geese, harsh and exciting –
over and over announcing your place
in the family of things.

—Mary Oliver

Discussion Questions for Mindfulness Reading

1. How do the first five lines of the poem connect the way we treat our bodies to our emotions?

2. Circle words in the poem that relate to wellness. What advice does this poem give about being well?

3. One main idea of the poem is your connection to everything in the universe. What is one way you can connect to nature, others, animals, and so forth to improve your overall wellness?

QUOTATION TO CONTEMPLATE

"Health is a state of body.
Wellness is a state of being."

(J. Stanford)

1. What does this quotation mean literally?

2. What is its deeper meaning?

3. What personal connections do you have with the quotation?

12

CULTIVATING A HEALTHY MINDSET

Lots of thoughts run through your head every day, some that you might not even be completely aware of. Mindfulness has the power to draw attention to these thoughts and help you take stock of the things you are telling yourself. It can also afford you a greater sense of freedom to make the changes you would like in your life. How you think can affect your happiness and wellness, so it's important to tune in.

Stanford University psychology professor Carol Dweck came up with an idea known as *growth mindset*, or an internal belief system that it is possible to grow and develop, particularly in school. This is in contrast to a *fixed mindset* or internal belief system that it is not possible to grow and develop, that one is born, for example, either smart or stupid. This chapter will help you develop healthy thought patterns and belief systems so that instead of being ruled by your brain, you can get it to work for you.

SELF-ASSESSMENT

Circle your response to the question below.

How calm are you, on a scale from 1 to 10, with 1 being very stressed and 10 being very calm?

1   2   3   4   5   6   7   8   9   10

What thoughts or feelings did you notice when reading the introduction to this chapter or filling out this self-assessment question? If you'd like, feel free to get more specific by writing or drawing what is going on for you in school and life right now:

DRIFT AWAY

It is important to know what is swirling around in your brain. The goal of this exercise is to help you tune in and identify your thoughts. This may or may not be a pleasant experience, but identifying a particularly negative thought can be helpful in learning to let it go. Fill in the clouds below with thoughts that you think are not serving you (helping you). Examples of such thoughts are: "I am a failure" or "I will never make it to Thanksgiving break!" How do the thoughts you wrote down make you feel? When you have written your thoughts in the clouds, take a deep breath in, and on the exhale, imagine each thought drifting away.

CREATE AN AFFIRMATION

An affirmation is an encouraging statement that you can repeat to yourself or post somewhere you'll see it often, like on a Post-it on your mirror. The word *affirmation* comes from the Latin *affirmare*, originally meaning "to make steady, strengthen." Writing affirmations can steady and strengthen your thoughts, giving you good focus and energy for classes, social activities, and homework. Find an affirmation below that resonates with you today and highlight it. Then write your own affirmation.

- ► I've got what I need to be successful inside me already!
- ► When I am _____, I am safe. (Examples: in my room, watching movies, happy).
- ► People act based on their own struggles and issues.
- ► It is okay to feel whatever I am feeling right now.
- ► I deserve joy and happiness every day of my life.
- ► My failures help develop my creativity.
- ► I don't need _____ (money, vacations, hateful people) to be happy.
- ► I am in school for _____ (myself, my kids, etc.).
- ► If I am tired, I will do my best to sleep.
- ► I am in charge of how I spend my time.
- ► I can do this.

Your Affirmation:

CHANGE THE MESSAGE

Sometimes the messages we tell ourselves are not accurate, but with repetition, we start to believe they are true. By shifting our self-talk we can change the pattern of negative, inaccurate thinking and instead learn to uplift ourselves. On the cell phones below, write an inaccurate, negative message you have been telling yourself beside each angry emoticon. Then write a message that is more accurate beside each happy emoticon.

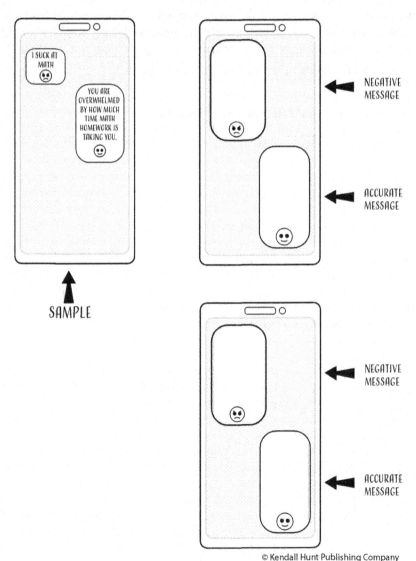

MINDSET

A mindset is how you think about things, the lens you use to look at situations, so to speak. For example, if you have an optimistic mindset, you might think that even though you didn't get a ton of sleep last night, you can still pass a test. If you have a less optimistic mindset, you might think that there is no way to pass.

For you, what does an *unhealthy* mindset look like? Does it mean giving up easily? Saying negative things to yourself? Blaming others for things that go wrong? What does a *healthy* mindset look like? Respect for others? Growing through failures? Something else? Describe healthy and unhealthy mindsets below using words or pictures.

Unhealthy Mindset Description or Pictures

Healthy Mindset Description or Pictures

MINDFULNESS READING

Excerpt from **"Ah, But the Breezes"** by Noelle Oxenhandler

Yet something remarkable happens when we go on sitting through all the *but*'s, through all the thoughts, sensations, and emotions that we would so like to oust. Gradually they begin to feel less alien, less like *obstacles* in the way, rocks in the path. Our deepening awareness becomes a kind of dew, falling on everything equally, allowing everything to sparkle. Once, in the midst of a meditation retreat, a friend went for a walk in the woods and found to her amazement that the litter was beautiful. Rusty cans, a beer bottle lying on pine needles: Everything was shining like a jewel.

Discussion Questions for Mindfulness Reading

1. What does Oxenhandler mean when she says "sitting through all the *but*'s"?

2. Why do you think that the author was able to see the litter in the woods as beautiful? Have you ever had an experience like this?

3. If you are having a hard time in school or life, do you block out your struggles, or do you try to understand them? Explain.

QUOTATION TO CONTEMPLATE

"Whatever action you take in a state of inner resistance (which we could also call negativity) will create more outer resistance, and the universe will not be on your side; life will not be helpful. If the shutters are closed, the sunlight cannot come in."

(Eckhart Tolle from *A New Earth*)

1. What does this quotation mean literally?

2. What is its deeper meaning?

3. What personal connections do you have with the quotation?

13

USING TECHNOLOGY MINDFULLY

You cannot escape technology! It infiltrates all parts of your life and the education system, now more than ever. Though some technology has immense benefits, there are also negative consequences of using too much technology. This chapter aims to focus awareness on the ways you use technology, the amount of time you spend on it, and the pros and cons of screen time. Exercises like taking a break from screens and finding positive uses for technology can help you reflect on your personal relationship with this important tool.

SELF-ASSESSMENT

Circle your response to the question below.

How calm are you, on a scale from 1 to 10, with 1 being very stressed and 10 being very calm?

1   2   3   4   5   6   7   8   9   10

What thoughts or feelings did you notice when reading the introduction to this chapter or filling out this self-assessment question? If you'd like, feel free to get more specific by writing or drawing what is going on for you in school and life right now:

SCREEN TIME-OUT

Using your phone makes your brain send out dopamine, which creates a sense of pleasure. It's no wonder that so many people are addicted to technology. It is important to have pleasure in your life, but balance is key with screen time. In this activity, you are going to take some time away from your screens. The idea is not to deprive yourself of pleasure, though. First, make a list of four activities that you find pleasurable that you might do when you want to mindlessly reach for your phone, turn on Netflix, or scroll social media.

Activities to replace technology use:

1.

2.

3.

4.

The next time you are motivated to use a screen, say the following to yourself: "I am looking for pleasure. This is normal. Today I'm going to try a new activity." Then engage in one of the replacement activities you wrote above. Write how it went in the box below. Would you be motivated to try another Screen Time-Out? Why or why not?

MAKE A LIST: TECHNOLOGY

Because we use technology so much in our daily lives, it's important to mindfully examine our relationship to different technologies and how they affect our well-being. Make two lists below to explore this further. (It is possible that the same technology might appear on both lists.)

List 1: Technology That Boosts My Happiness

List 2: Technology That Creates Stress in My Life

WELL-BEING APP

In an effort to support people's well-being and use technology in a positive way, developers have created numerous well-being apps. From meditation to increasing happiness to tracking health, many free apps are available. Download a well-being app to your device and reflect on it below. You can search for a category like wellness, mindfulness, or happiness wherever you get your apps, and see what pops up. You could also ask for recommendations from friends or Internet searches.

What app did you download?

Why did you choose this app?

If you've begun using it, what do you find useful about it?

POSITIVE MEME

Memes infiltrate many of the technologies you use daily, from social media to texting to online learning platforms. One way to help balance your mental health with technology use is to make sure the content you encounter is positive and uplifting. Do your part to create a more positive online world by creating a meme that spreads a positive message. Then share it with others. Brainstorm your meme ideas below.

MINDFULNESS READING

Haiku
by Barry George

moonlit
our cell phones charging
side by side

wee hours hospital ward—
one of those beeps
and boops is me

city of phones—
the lost art
of talking to oneself

Copyright © Barry George. Reprinted by permission. Barry George's poetry collections include *Sirens and Rain* (Accents Publishing), *Wrecking Ball and Other Urban Haiku* (Accents Publishing) and *The One That Flies Back* (Kattywompus Press).

Discussion Questions for Mindfulness Reading

1. How do these three poems show the connection between humans and technology?

2. How do they show the disconnection between humans and technology?

3. Imagine hanging out with your friend without your phones. How might leaving the phones behind change your interaction?

MEDITATION BEFORE USING SOCIAL MEDIA

Complete this meditation before logging on to social media. Choose someone to read it aloud or simply read it to yourself. Pause for a few seconds between sentences.

Begin by centering yourself in the present moment. Look around and name three things you see. Close your eyes and listen to the noises around you without judgment. Then notice that you are breathing.

Imagine it is raining positivity wherever you are. Feel the drops fall on you. Let them sink in to your innermost being.

Focusing again on your breath, breathe deep down into that positivity. And then exhale the positivity out into the space around you. Notice that sharing positivity does not take it away from you. Instead, it multiplies the good energy in your space.

May you recognize the positivity you have to share. May you realize the unique gifts you bring to the world. You need not compare yourself to anyone, for you possess a positivity of your own making. You shine with your own brilliant light.

When you are ready, open your eyes and connect to the space around you. Then log onto social media and breathe your light into that online space.

14

LOOKING AHEAD

Is it possible to be mindful and rooted in the present, while also being aware of and excited about your future? Of course! College is all about working in the now to gain the tools you need to have a successful and happy future. As your semester draws to a close, this is the perfect time to dream about where you're headed next and keep positive momentum flowing into your next semester.

SELF-ASSESSMENT

Circle your response to the question below.

How calm are you, on a scale from 1 to 10, with 1 being very stressed and 10 being very calm?

1 2 3 4 5 6 7 8 9 10

What thoughts or feelings did you notice when reading the introduction to this chapter or filling out this self-assessment question? If you'd like, feel free to get more specific by writing or drawing what is going on for you in school and life right now:

PATH TO POSSIBILITIES

While dreaming about the future, it is equally important to recognize your accomplishments so far. What milestones have you achieved so far in your educational journey? What are your future goals (in school and beyond)? Draw them on the path below!

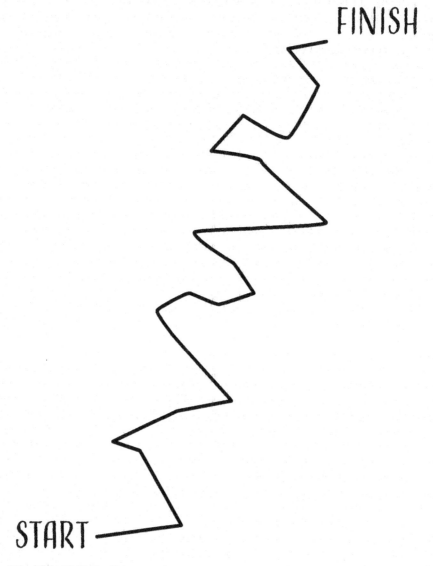

FINISH

START

TEACH!

One of the best ways to sharpen a skill is to share it with others. Teach a mindfulness practice that you have learned to someone you know. You can do this by explaining a concept or asking the person to do an activity in this book!

Write down the name of the person you will teach here:

What will you teach them?

How did it go? (Write this after you teach them.)

NETWORK!

Your network is your web of relationships, and networking means growing this web. Because your relationships with others can help you in your career and in your future, big networking events like college job fairs can be very helpful. When you talk to a teacher about a career goal, that is also networking. When you ask a friend if they know anyone in your field and then e-mail that person, that's networking too! Building a network is not just about knowing a person but also letting that person know and respect *you* a bit. For example, you are likely to hear about a job opportunity from someone who knows you are looking and thinks you might be a good fit. Take a moment to center, and then answer the questions below about networking:

1. Have you ever networked before? Talk about that experience. Was it easy or hard for you? If you have not yet networked, why haven't you?

2. What might be one way to network mindfully? Think about what you have learned about mindfulness practice; there is no right or wrong answer to this question.

3. Look up an event related to your major or career and then write what it is and when it is. Would you like to attend this event? Explain.

DIPLOMA MANDALA

A mandala is a patterned shape that represents a small piece of the universe. The ritual of coloring mandalas can help focus your attention. In the squares below, write your name and/or the names of others you hope will graduate from college. Then, color the mandala. Notice any thoughts or feelings that come up for you as you complete this activity.

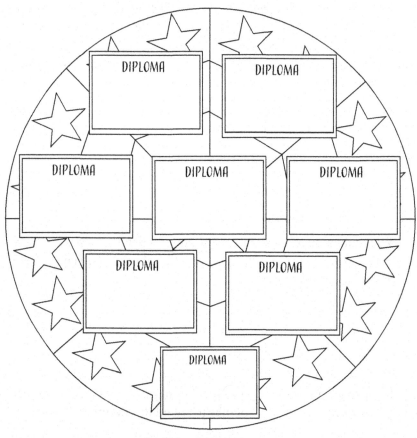

© Kendall Hunt Publishing Company

DREAMS

Color the Eleanor Roosevelt quotation below. Then write or discuss whether or not you believe that your dreams are beautiful. What is one step you can take today toward achieving your dreams?

Image adapted © Shutterstock.com

QUOTATION TO CONTEMPLATE

"Let yourself be silently drawn by
the stronger pull of what you really love."

(Rumi)

1. What does this quotation mean literally?

2. What is its deeper meaning?

3. What personal connections do you have with the quotation?

15

REFLECTING

One of the most important life lessons you can glean from college is the power of reflection. No matter how much you learn and change, it will not have as much meaning unless you draw awareness to this growth. The end of the semester is exhausting, but it is essential to find some small moments to reflect. Mindfulness will help you pause before moving on to the next semester or the next big thing.

SELF-ASSESSMENT

Circle your response to the question below.

How calm are you, on a scale from 1 to 10, with 1 being very stressed and 10 being very calm?

1 2 3 4 5 6 7 8 9 10

What thoughts or feelings did you notice when reading the introduction to this chapter or filling out this self-assessment question? If you'd like, feel free to get more specific by writing or drawing what is going on for you in school and life right now:

NOTE TO SELF

Reflecting on the semester as a whole can help you recognize how you've grown and all you've accomplished. Think back to the start of this semester, and write a letter to yourself at that time. Use the space below.

MAKE A LIST:
FIVE THINGS YOU LEARNED THIS SEMESTER

You are probably aware that you learned a lot this semester. However, writing down what you learned helps you process your growth in a more direct way. Make a list of five things you learned this semester in the space below. You might want to focus on academic things you've learned, but also feel free to branch out into ways you've grown as an individual.

1.

2.

3.

4.

5.

MIRROR, MIRROR

While looking yourself in the eyes in a mirror, repeat an affirmation you wrote this semester. You could also write a new affirmation for this exercise, based on your personal growth this semester.

Write the affirmation here:

TRANSFORMATION

As you know, butterflies go through an extreme transformation from caterpillar to colorful, ethereal butterfly. Humans also undergo transformations like this internally. As you color, reflect about a transformative experience and the insights you gained from that experience.

Images adapted © Shutterstock.com

MINDFULNESS READING

Excerpt from **"Why You Should Make Time for Reflecting (Even if You Hate Doing It)"** by Jennifer Porter.

Reflection gives the brain an opportunity to pause amidst the chaos, untangle and sort through observations and experiences, consider multiple possible interpretations, and create meaning. This meaning becomes learning, which can then inform future mindsets and actions.

Discussion Questions for Mindfulness Reading

1. How does reflection help a person find meaning?

2. What mindfulness techniques do you think would work best for your own reflection process?

3. What meaning have you taken away from this semester?

QUOTATION TO CONTEMPLATE

"Things which do not grow
and change are dead things."

(Louise Erdrich)

1. What does this quotation mean literally?

2. What is its deeper meaning?

3. What personal connections do you have with the quotation?

JOURNAL PAGES

JOURNAL PAGES

ABOUT THE AUTHORS

ELIZABETH CATANESE

Elizabeth Catanese is an associate professor of English at Community College of Philadelphia. Trained in mindfulness-based stress reduction, Elizabeth has enjoyed incorporating mindfulness activities into her college classroom for the past ten years. Elizabeth works to deepen her mindful awareness through writing children's books, cartooning, and parenting her energetic twin toddlers, Dylan and Escher.

KATE SANCHEZ

Kate Sanchez is an assistant professor of English at Community College of Philadelphia, where she enjoys finding creative ways to incorporate mindfulness into her curriculum. Inspired by her own journey, she created the Vitamin.K.mindful YouTube channel to share mindful living strategies with others. She is a certified meditation and mindfulness teacher through the School of Positive Transformation. Every night before bed, she does a metta "lovingkindness" meditation with her toddler daughter.

Works Cited

Bailey, Elizabeth Tova. *The Sound of a Wild Snail Eating*. Algonquin, 2016.

Beattie, Melody. "Gratitude." *MelodyBeattie.com*, https://melodybeattie. com/gratitude-2/. Accessed 14 May 2021.

Bechdel, Alison. *Fun Home: A Family Tragicomic*. Mariner, 2007.

Brooks, David. "What Suffering Does." *The New York Times*, 7 Apr. 2014, https://www.nytimes.com/2014/04/08/opinion/brooks-what-suffering-does.html. Accessed 12 May 2021.

Cather, Willa. "Prairie Spring." *Poets.org*, Academy of American Poets, https://poets.org/poem/prairie-spring. Accessed 12 May 2021.

Coates, Ta-Nehisi. *Between the World and Me*. Spiegel & Grau, 2015.

Coelho, Paulo. *The Alchemist*, Translated by Alan R. Clarke, Perfection Learning, 2006.

Covey, Stephen R. *The 7 Habits of Highly Effective People: Powerful Lessons in Personal Change*. Simon & Schuster, 2013.

Doyle, Arthur Conan. *The Adventures of Sherlock Holmes: A Case of Identity*. CreateSpace Independent, 2016.

Dweck, Carol S. *Mindset: The New Psychology of Success*. Ballantine, 2007.

George, Barry. *Sirens and Rain*. Accents, 2020.

---. *The One That Flies Back*. Kattywompus, 2015.

---. *Wrecking Ball & Other Urban Haiku*. Accents, 2010.

Himeles, Darla. *Flesh Enough*. Get Fresh Books, 2017.

Homer. *The Odyssey*, Translated by Samuel Butler, *Project Gutenberg*, 1999, https://www.gutenberg.org/files/1727/1727-h/1727-h.htm. Accessed 4 May 2021.

Jung, Carl Gustav. *Psychological Reflections: A New Anthology of His Writings 1905-61*, edited by Jolande Jacobi. Routledge, 1986.

Kabat-Zinn, Jon. *Wherever You Go There You Are*. Hyperion, 1994.

Keng, S., et al. "Effects of Mindfulness on Psychological Health: A Review of Empirical Studies." *Clinical Psychology Review*, vol. 31, no. 6, 2011, http://www.ncbi.nlm.nih.gov/pmc/articles/PMC3679190/. Accessed 3 May 2021.

Law, Ingrid. *Savvy*. Puffin, 2010.

Mendelson, T., et al. "Feasibility and preliminary outcomes of a school-based mindfulness intervention for urban youth." *Journal of Abnormal Child Psychology*, vol. 38, 2010, https://link.springer.com/article/10.1007/s10802-010-9418-x. Accessed 3 May 2021.

Merriam-Webster.com. Merriam-Webster, https://www.merriam-webster.com. Accessed 4 May 2021.

Oliver, Mary. *Dream Work*. Atlantic Monthly, 1986.

Oxenhandler, Noelle. "Ah, But the Breezes. . . ." *Tricycle*, The Buddhist Review, https://tricycle.org/magazine/ah-breezes/. Accessed 1 May 2021.

Porter, Lavelle. "Dear Sister Outsider: On Audre Lorde and writing oneself into existence." *Poetry Foundation*, https://www.poetryfoundation.org/articles/89445/dear-sister-outsider. Accessed 14 May 2021.

Rosenthal, Norman E. "Using Meditation to Help Close the Achievement Gap." *Well New York Times Blog*, 2016, http://well.blogs.nytimes.com/2016/06/02/. Accessed 3 May 2021.

Rumi, Jalal al-Din. *The Essential Rumi*, Translated by Coleman Barks, HarperOne, 2004.

Thoreau, Henry David. *Walden*. CreateSpace Independent, 2018.

Tolle, Eckhart. *A New Earth: Awakening to Your Life's Purpose*. Penguin, 2008.

---. *The Power of Now: A Guide to Spiritual Enlightenment*. New World Library, 2004.

"What is Mindfulness?" *Mindfulness in Schools Project*, https://mindfulnessinschools.org/mindfulness/. Accessed 3 May 2021.

Whitman, Walt. *Leaves of Grass. Project Gutenberg,* https://www.
gutenberg.org/files/1322/1322-h/1322-h.htm. Accessed 13 May 2021.

Yousafzai, Malala. *I Am Malala: The Girl Who Stood Up For Education
And Was Shot By The Taliban.* Confer Books, 2015.